Past Lives

Past Lives

Leah Dodd

TE HERENGA WAKA
UNIVERSITY PRESS

Te Herenga Waka University Press
Victoria University of Wellington
PO Box 600 Wellington
teherengawakapress.co.nz

A catalogue record is available at the National Library
of New Zealand.

ISBN 9781776920686

Printed in Singapore by Markono Print Media Pte Ltd

for Asa

Contents

2

1

soulmates

last night I locked eyes   with a possum
its gaze moon-dark   and gleaming
        through the bedroom window

it trying to get in
        me trying to get out

I wished so hard   for us to switch
            we could parent-trap this baby
        I offered the possum

it could   make breakfast
        and sleep   in my bed

I could   run night wild
        get to know   mother nature

/

on the street   back when it was safe
        to speak to each other
                a passing student

took out an earbud
            to say   *you guys just look so gorgeous!*

I was carrying three litres of milk
        like a braided   full-lipped maiden
and J was carrying   the baby

I am as gorgeous as   a deadly chameleon
or   a 'beware of the dog' sign
tattooed   on a lower back

11

I am as gorgeous as   a vat of green slime
ready to be   poured
        over a group   of unsuspecting
regional schoolchildren

this? I wanted to say   to the student
        forehead to forehead   preferably
holding their shoulders   in a grip of wisdom

this is a lake of magma
and I am sinking further every day

/

the possum and I kept staring
        neither of us   wanting to blink
in case the moment   shattered

I was reaching out an arm   at a glacial pace
        to open the window   and
consummate   the bond

when a car   hooned   through the valley below
        blasting   a dub remix
            of 'Hot Potato' by the Wiggles

all the way up   to my sweet new friend
        whose eyes grew   dinner-plate wide

        and in the same moment
            it scampered away
    to the black undergrowth
behind
    the lighted path

spawning season

all the rainbow trout are packed into the smallest river ever. a creek, really, and you might think *wow can they even breathe* before you remember the first thing about fish. they seem so slippery and genderless that you almost envy them, before you remember that most, especially the ones in this lake, will be caught and killed by White Men with Holiday Homes. the creek is so clear, with a quaint cobbled bridge, which brings to mind southern France, where you've never been, and makes you want to take a big breath in and say *ahhh*. you could watch them all day, these trout, rubbing up against one another like straight girls at the gay bar, laying their eggs and swimming towards a Better Place. you can almost hear their husky trout voices: *sorry hon* and *scuse me Tina* and *behind!* you wonder which of them likes to stir the pot or say to salmon *I've lived here for fifteen years fine with none of your kind around and I won't be told what to do by one of yours thank you very much*. probably none. you really could watch them all day, but it's the middle of winter and your boyfriend came all this way to the holiday log cabin only to stoke fires and get sick and he's busy puking up and taking too many cold & flu tablets and you're starting to worry, so you better go back in actually, you better go make him a hot chocolate or rub his back.

Mt Eden 2005

on rosewood floors
the sisters unspool around
candles and beaded cushions

three-quarter cargos rolled high
they spread sugary wax like butter
over the peaks of their shins

the youngest dresses
baby dolls in blue onesies
and rocks them to sleep

the sisters squeeze each other's
back pimples and sing Leonard Cohen
in four-part harmony to their mother

and feed her toast with tomato and salt
since an article online said it might
help with the tumour

this room has the bay window
and outside are mansions
and car lights and Venus

they share stories in blushed voices
as the candles burn down
each face an open violet

once the wax dries, they grip
between thumb and finger
and quickly they pull

when you want to be a mermaid so bad it hurts

peel the lid from a tin of tuna   lick the oily brine for breakfast   think *mermaid*
     mermaid   *mermaid*   hard as you can   imagine your voice
a sweet sea bell   chiming through the deep   legs fused shut how
     graceful it would be   to arc   through black water

*

the dress-up box has no tail   only   white platform Pulps   a veil
     (tattered, nylon)   a long, beaded skirt that might   be called *ethnic*
on TradeMe   and a cap-sleeved rainbow leotard   once worn   in a half-hearted
     attempt   at ballet   with a slicked bun   and
          a glum   twirl   across the school hall stage

*

pick the leotard and skirt   push your hair back   with a black crochet headband
     press iridescent glitter   to the parts of your face   that light hits
and lie still   in the garden   bake   under January sun
     your painfully human body   over grass   over earth   over
eight buried pet rats   gassed   in blue ice-cream tubs   once they became
     old, arthritic   twist   your two legs around each other
watch them snake   against the green   *mermaid*   *mermaid*
     mermaid   like Cher   like Winona   like 2D Disney in primary
colours   the dashing prince   the red crab   the black storm

*

they are wondering where you are   but inside there's   that kitchen   that
     open door   they are wondering where you are   the clouds have
clotted   like a bruise   behind the kauri   they are wondering
where you are   but it's hard to breathe when   the gills of your neck need
          water   it's hard to be heard when you   sing
in undersea frequencies   stay out   a little longer   watch the sun
     dip   behind the tree you have seen   every day   of your small mortal life

masterclass

1

one night   seventeen
got high   listened to *Ummagumma* on repeat
then fell in a pool   and floated

the next morning   a masterclass
      at the Catholic school   nearly fell
into the gutter   getting out of the car

the pianist was young   a prodigy
used to have a ponytail   he loved Schumann
and lived in Berlin   or somewhere like Berlin

I sat at the piano   faced the crowd
      of ballet flats   and polar fleece
opened to Romance   Op. 28 No. 2 in F# major

and pressed into the notes   the song that sat snug
in the middle of three staves   the piece
    split   in three   that moves as one

2

Schumann once spoke   of a summer afternoon
    the beauty   of nature   in silence

pull back he said   when I hinged on the double-sharp
the ternary's   turbulent middle   and slid back
    into treble

    pull back

I was only a vessel   a tide pool
               clear salt water
       full of small creatures   that batten
                                                     down
               into their shells
         when   the rain comes

3

the landlord upstairs teaches piano till 9
by then   the sky is so black
                    you could drown in it

I've got plenty of students so   you might hear them
        I'm thinking of cutting down
he said   flicking away lint

I remember the pianist telling me
                         to think of the song
               in the middle
         like a lullaby

like I'm singing a baby to sleep

I remember the way he balled his fist
                    under my wrist
         and said

    tender   tender   tender

like you could make it sound
      a certain way
            just by saying the word

'Patched gang members in the Māori Affairs Committee Room', 1979

said her dad was a mob boss
busy saving lives that's why he's been
gone since she was little

her mum stood doorway small
holding their pet chicken
and laughed and laughed

then *if that's what you think*
eh sweets and gave us deep-fried
chips and a crystal for the sun

*

on their street you drove
doors locked windows up
the region bracketed blue and red

in this city you either ate
shroom sandwiches in parking lots
or had a family bach in Raglan

sometimes these lives bleed together
like last year when a holiday kid
found a body in a river

*

after seeing the photo (black and white
soft light subtle grain)
I thought of teachers with stories

of glass-bottled milk delivered free
that sat outside all day in large crates
and made them sick

I thought of Mrs O. lining up lyrics
to 'Octopus's Garden' under the projector
and making kapa haka optional

*

at Farmers
gang members tried flirting
their way into discounts

but they had nothing on Deb
department manager
with her coke nail and lung cancer

who once cornered me in the break room
by the Nescafé tin and said birth control
doesn't work babe trust me I got five kids

*

the council blasts Debussy
and Mozart loud
outside the library

where brown kids linger
and drink and fight
like white culture down the throat

I think of the film roll
that surrounds this photo
forever peopled and silent

*

in other shots a barefoot man
moons the lens
and a mutton-chopped mob member

holds baby and bottle
while here in the committee room
a broad back reads HEAD HUNTERS

over a flaming skull
and the sun glows in
through the carvings

guided hypnosis

you are at a country piss-up   the cows and horses have gone to sleep   the garage
walls are made of Fleetwood Mac   you have had just enough whisky and put
yourself to bed in your boyfriend's king single   with the pastel wool blanket
and second-hand duvet   that smells of skin and cum   but in a nice way   like
getting your period when you   have no plans   and you've treated yourself
by turning on the heat pump   and there's a   jug on the boil
all set to be fed into a hotty   the garage light seeps under the door
like heaven   you can still hear Stevie but   it's fine you'll sleep easy
knowing that your boyfriend is still running round the garage   in nothing but his
threadbare undies   and a motorbike helmet

you puked in the sleep-out toilet like eighteen months ago   everyone joked that
you had to clean it   but they weren't joking   and nobody cleaned it and the little
chunks have crystallised   stuck on for good   like diamantés hot-glue-gunned
onto a denim jacket   you kind of don't mind   it means that nobody will forget
you were there   like how bears grind all up on trees in spring

you wonder if your boyfriend will   go to piss soon   and think of you   he lost his
voice after *Blood on the Tracks* and now   is doing his best to croak along to 'Tusk'
as sleep sneaks closer   like a debt collector or the tooth fairy   those tom-toms beat
into your brain   hypnotic   your boyfriend is probably   wiggling his bits
in his friend's   sister's face again   hips in orbit   o how he loves to cut a rug

you'll have a talk with him tomorrow   in front of the fire maybe   after the fifth
action movie maybe over a mince pie and a Just Juice bubbles   his vocal fry beams
through the walls   *JUST SAY THAT YOU WANT ME*   there it is   gorgeous
a snow-globe set to life   all sound is the gold strip of light under the door
you take a long breath   snuggle deep   tomorrow   you'll feel even better

West Coast School of Rock

it was a time of *Empire Records* and *The Runaways*
black miniskirts and steel-capped boots
gigs at an emptied warehouse
where kids learnt riffs and
soaked their black tees with sweat

System of a Down chewed through the PA
even during the set but nobody noticed or cared
even when teen bones cracked in a wall
of death she stood like Moses
and surrendered

when the door sucked open for a smoke
he squinted at December sun
shook out legs and knuckles
then rolled a thin spliff

hand around wrist he led her
behind a shipping container

the sky bared stars
his fingers traced
up and down her arm

girls like this sometimes

on the damp bank behind them
his western belt
his torn-up 501s

his breath smelled of smoke and mint
and met the dark air in small clouds

pining over Venus later that night
from the bedroom window
a grainy photo landed on her phone:
half a stick-and-poked J
(for Jim Morrison)

on his left ass cheek
that hurt too much to finish

tramping

I was clueless about your little gas stove
I would've eaten those packet curries cold

we drew cards by candlelight
had quick sex while we were alone
pale skin stuck to blue
plastic canvas that shone
under mountain light

we went to bed with full bladders
because the long drop where flies
kissed both cheeks and the swampy
dark walk to get there
was so unholy

a youth group sang worship songs
all night
and then played truth or dare
but not the way we did

Memphis Belle

the barista asked if I wanted sugar / I quoted Shakespeare between sips /
we were young thespians / in the big smoke / for a Shakespeare fest /
in Pigeon Park we sat close and gripped single-use cups / like small treasures

when we ate I only bought sides / cos a teacher said I looked great in those Jeffrey
Campbells from Recycle Boutique / he was cool and shopped at Hunters &
Collectors so / I spent $40 to clog around / vaguely starving for five whole days

I tried to put false lashes on P / who was so trusting / glue dripped into her eyes /
we were scared she'd go blind / right before we went on / she squinted lines at me
through wet black lashes / I think it added a *je ne sais quoi* to the tone

all night VACANCY flashed into our room / we looked at each other on metal
bunks / B said she was trained in Chinese massage / she was lying and really
messed up my back / I was too timid to say stop this is awful

in the morning our American teacher / who mocked us for saying *Bonne eye-va*
instead of *Bon Iver* / turned and clipped her bra across freckled skin /
then went to complain about the sign

we wore the most interesting clothes we had / I wore a cream fur coat everywhere /
even though it was barely autumn / and nobody looked at us because
we weren't back home / we were just kids anyway / what's to see

0800 SEE ORCA

we had nothing left   to love
         only   our vacuum cleaners
and loyal toasters

we couldn't halt   the emissions
           or save   the western
      black rhinos   so
we refreshed web pages
                  and watched
          as Peter Jackson
      made   a special teat

and watched
      in disbelief   as they began to say
           rapidly deteriorating
      and
           died in the sea pen

*

the night birds   are arguing
one kākā probably screeching   to another
      that   *orcas aren't even whales*
they're actually   *dolphins*   *who were called*
    'whale killers'   *but the phrase*
mutated   *over time*   *like 'Yeshua' to 'Jesus'*
        until   *it meant*
    something else
        entirely

•

on the bus I pass the nail salon
      a girl stares blankly
           out the window
is she
      in mourning too?

I want to call the orca hotline
      set up   to collect
pod-sighting information
      and   send my condolences
I want to
      offer warmth, thoughts
maybe even   recite a poem

I want to have   empathetic
      grief-infused phone sex
with the operator
      surely   they'll know
          how I am feeling
I want to scream

I want to scream
      down the orca hotline
HOW COULD YOU LET THIS HAPPEN

I want to know
      where the baby's family is
         if they miss him
if they
went back to look

bus poem 1

someone with candyfloss-coloured hair
cradles two litres of milk in their arms

a silver four-wheeler rears past
water spinning off tyres

drivers steer their vessels
into the gusty unknown

a brown-haired baby gives me the side eye
I give it back but like   in a funny way

I wasn't dressed for this weather
my cheap wool won't stand the blue rain

I am ejected with a *whoosh*
and a loud closing door

wind stings my neck like a love bite
and the first thing I see is a wishbone

picked clean like the trees
cleaving air   landing in the gutter

I'm losing leaves too   soon I'll have none left
          my bed is full of them   every morning

                    I shake out the sheets

and leaves rot in a layer on the floor

clot

in the shower
a blood clot in the shape
of Aotearoa floats
near my feet
then slides
South-Island-first
to the drain

I wonder what shape
my first baby
would have been
and if I would have
recognised
a limb, a likeness,
a human part

before
being swept
away in the flush
of bowl
to pipe
and eventually
ocean

tether

we're doing it all together! eating
brown rice porridge, washing
dishes doing laundry, watching
a poor dead blackbird's feathers
ruffling gently outside   we can see
honeysuckle growing out
of concrete   smell its sweet air
see the washing lines twist   punctuated
with pegs   around each other

baby blows raspberries, shrieks
we fizz and hiss together! we dance
to 'Heart of Glass'   & he watches me
cry, confused, when we listen to Big Thief
we can hear singing birds
marking death in our yard

we are cutting front teeth, howling
when they burst through pink gum
somehow . . .   together
our fingers trace pictures of piglets
chicks, kittens   I kiss the crown
of his head, he squeals   wriggles away
eyes set on the cat's black tail

he'll cry if I leave   little limpet
but oh, I love the closeness   it slips
so quickly   once we were connected
by a vein and two arteries   ever since
we drift   I take these gifts with grace

I am a moonscape of blood and kitchen grit
ultraviolet bone & blotted sleep   one day
we will be separate creatures
I will give kitchen scissor haircuts
tether balloons on a string to a wrist
wrap birthday presents in the witching hour
and became a different animal altogether

clucky

in poems, babies are like snacks –
doughy loaves, apple-cheeked,
sweet as pie, sausage-toed

victim to the metaphor,
I call my peach-fuzzed baby *yummy*
because he is so tasty
I could just toss him in olive oil
and roll him into a kebab

I had a friend who kept six kittens
in a cardboard box

I had to physically stop her from nibbling
their tiny grey ears off because
they were so cute she
couldn't help herself

and this is similar,
the sweet milky smell of brand-new skin,
those pillowy cloud-nine cheeks,
the tiny hands –

it's a perfect storm
like looking over the edge of a cliff,
arms full of candied apples
and velvet ruby hearts

muscle memory

By the time we are barefoot and dancing to Gwen Stefani on damp carpet,
we're friends again.

Peach soju spills on my secondhand skirt. In my palm the tambourine bleeds
silver discs. She

flicks through sticky songs, bans the Beatles. I remember doing lines in her cold
apartment, nudged neat

with her library card. For the rest of that night I spoke only French, and called my
ex at dawn.

I know each step of the path home and make sure to drink a litre of water
once I'm in.

The baby wakes up at 7 and I groan back into the world. I make toast. I wash nappies.
I hold him

close, sing 'High Tide or Low Tide'. He goes down for his nap and I go down
for mine. Later,

I find a Stevie Nicks top for $6 at Vinnies that retails for $200. I try it on but in the
fitting room light

it hangs sad on my bruised body. I don't know which clothes suit the
shape of me,

and I don't know anyone with a feijoa tree, one growing so much fruit that they
bring it over

and say take it, I can't eat all this, which is still the best way I know to
measure my loneliness.

bus poem 2

someone told me about the carbon footprint
     of an email
         but I can't remember

what they compared it to
only
   that it was bad

       and that we should all
stop using the internet

everything's a little lost
in translation these days

I wonder what my *thank you driver*
would sound like without face mask & headphones

/

last night after stalking the Royals' Instagram accounts
I dreamed Prince Harry was a distant cousin

and we sat together on an armchair
with soft cream upholstery, gold accents

and cherrywood frame just wide
enough for my hips next to his

he gave me a collection of art prints,
Rothko, Monet, maybe a Matisse

drawing them out of a little tote
one by one like a magic trick

/

then I was on a bus that crashed
but we all survived   (I think)

it was somewhere between Brooklyn and Newtown
the wheels swerved around a corner

missed the road and
sent the bus tumbling

off a cliff through dense bush
down
        down
                down

/

there was screaming, of course
and at the bottom we all sort of just
                                piled out
                brushed ourselves off
called loved ones

10,000 bees flew in
through the bus windows
like the sound of undivided light
and lifted the bus into the clouds

I clutched the tote full of art to my chest
took a deep breath
and started to clamber on mossy banks

only the groves of small trees
knew the way up

how to astral project in a rental bathroom

```
close your eyes        conjure a waterfall
don't think         of the slug trails
stretching across          the wall
watch steam         move like a spirit
watch the cheap          scented candle
its clouds of smoke       cut through
with coconut       peach-scented parabens
the silicon that slides        down the rope
of your hair           like a tiny firefighter
on a mission to tame       your middle-eastern genes
conjure the holy land         the olive trees
the children       you meet in your sleep
open                your third eye
your fourth!         conjure every layer
of the atmosphere                float up
until you balloon tight        and explode
into nothing            and once
you are nothing        rinse out
the herbal essences        and wring out
your hair          turn off the shower
and keep the fan on         until the room
has dried          completely
```

ilovekeats69

poets should have great, punchy

                                 passwords

     like   vaginawolfe3000

        or   poempoempoem6

passwords should include   a haiku, a hieroglyph

     and the blood

               of a virgin

but not

          in a *Jennifer's Body* sort of way

more in a cute   pixelated

             Minecraft way

every time a poet enters a password

                    a fairy should die

          I mean

they should be   reminded

            of why they write

and the reason is

     of course

for the lols

          it's always for the lols

          I know the lols

I was a child of the nineties

which means   I was 3 in the millennium

     so really I was   a child of

          the early 00s

which means

        my siblings dressed me up

in silver platform Pulps   and a wedding veil

which means   I remember dial-up

      oh   I remember
those slow melodic beeps
      each beep taking you closer
           to Club Penguin

I remember   the library-issued
           disc-drive games
where a sexy lion guides you
      through a castle and
         teaches you to read

      I was born knowing how to read
in fact   I was removed
from my mother's womb
with a copy of *Finnegan's Wake* in my hand
         yes   that's right

that's a lie
  but   I did read it
to impress a boy
who definitely had not
      read *Finnegan's Wake*

if I was a proper poet my password would be
rhymeordie1997
or internallyrhyming69

I would enter it into my Habbo Hotel account
and then   make my blocky lil avatar
      blonde and hot

inviting all the 'boys' n 'girls' to the rooftop
where we would lie parallel
      on a two-dimensional bed
and say things like *wat u wearin irl*

and *I lik ur huge titz*

there is a picture of me
sitting straight-backed at the computer desk
hand resting on the mouse as if
on the shoulder of a loved son

       I have the smile of a cool god
who just thought up   oil
and my hair is pushed back
      in a lilac headband
eyes heavy-lidded   even before
      the four-hour stint
   on Neopets

I am so pleased in this picture
it is as if I am bathing   in the warmth
      of unearthing   lost treasure
it is as if I am
     a long-ago queen
        being fed bits of
           early internet
like figs
     and magic wishes
on a silver tray

domestic goddess

I am tearing thighs apart with my bare hands
the rip   of raw flesh tries desperately
        to hold   itself together
but I am stronger than its dead wish   to stay intact
I am fuelled   by the flame of a thousand suns
        or whatever

take that, chicken   I whisper to the pink strips
        I rip   and I rip   and I rub it
in oil   cumin   paprika
        then I realise something
with the skeleton clarity   of a morning dream
yelling   over my shoulder   that
I have a lot of   ~violence~
        inside me   a lot of violence
that one might call   female rage

a term which   fills me with   more rage
which I take out   on the chicken

                imagine it's a man!
you yell back

only sort of listening   like a dog   ear half-cocked
        flinging the squealing baby   by his feet
                up and down   up and down

the Staple Singers fill the lounge
        the ferns outside   are thwacking the window
night is   preparing itself   for darkness

40

gig people

over there / the guy who threw beer like a baptism / into the heart of the King Gizzard crowd / the guy who bought four T-shirts at Connan Mockasin / and wore them all at once / soaking through each layer like a disease / the guy who came up at Moon and said *why you gotta look so hot playing keys I better come to more of your gigs* / there are so many armpits / pixie cuts and butterfly clips / thick prescription glasses / large woollen vests / mullets / bobs / kitchen scissors / body odour as communal as a co-op / beer stands / food trucks / lucky green lighters / craft beer in plastic cups / that cost $3 / the blackness in between / someone compliments my gold winged liner / we joke about the baby being home on his own / to three different people / the drummer plays like a rabid dog / brushes sweat / with the back of his hand / takes a breath after the last song and grins / like he's seen the deep belly of the beast / and lived

all the leaves are brown and my heart is a cage-free egg

shakshouka crackles   in the pan   whole yolks still glistening   olive oil sparks up
and spits   a northerly croon   tugs leaves   from the oak   they float
slow   through the air   to the street

.

I've been   drifting   through weeks   like a lapping tide
losing words to   the language   of cave   and clay banks
of pale green   bathwater   and beads   of cold sweat

.

the flower beds   have been gutted   turned fresh   ready
for hands   to push seeds   into   their dark   cocoon of soil   ready
to grow   into   something with   limbs   and colour

.

down on the footpath   a person in rust-coloured kick flares   dotted
lightly with rain   strides   to the soft beat   of traffic   dislodging from
their brown boot   what looks   like   a chicken nugget

.

my kitchen   smells of oil   smoke   and teen spirit   I have been thickening
growing taupe   in the cold   like   overnight oats   except lacking the
fun   toppings   the freeze-dried berries   and chia seeds

.

the open tub of compost   on the bench boasts an alp   of coffee grounds
eggshell   persimmon skins   and on top   a wedding cake couple   two shards
of pumpkin   dressed in olive-coloured mould   like   a couture suit

•

some days   all I do is   cut my fingernails   and   if it's going well   pay a bill
          gone are the days   I would grip   between my teeth   like
an orca   chasing seals   in the shallows   for no good reason

•

down on the street   local dogs trot   over thickets   of dead leaves returning
home with mouths full   of bracken   they have already forgotten
summer   its green chlorine stain   its ripe tangerines

•

one valley dog looks all the way   up here   meets my eye as if to say
          something like   *your hair looks nice tied up*   *with those tendrils*
          or   *hey*

     don't forget   *to rinse out that*   *crimson cast iron*
                              it's been
          in the sink
               for days and days

43

Last Call Nigel

when you were newborn
milk-drunk, eyes akimbo
koi mouth gaping

you were like an old man
downing his pint with sticky fingers
sinking to the bar like a ship

we called you Last Call Nigel
and he has made a comeback
this time swaggering, tottering

and other adjectives commonly used
to describe babies and drunk men
it's uncanny to see you upright –

we can't believe it! this clump of cells
this lentil-sized thing, this mango
in my pelvis can walk?! We say:

he's, like, a school-aged child!
he's . . . a first-year in halls!
he's Last Call Nigel again!

and then you are running, snatching
Apple chargers and poetry books
like forbidden fruit, and soon you will

jump   climb   skip

like the little imp you are

I am the ghost of the IKEA futon couch

here I am, hello!   fated to my corner   of the living room
     one ass cheek   flattened forever
        on two inches   of cushion

I don't remember what happened here   only   a melding
     moment   where bone and skin and tendons   fused
       with cotton, foam   steel frame

      it's probably for the best   this post-life haunting
I was never good at sport   I was only ever patriotic for Genovia

I kept showing up to things   just to be photographed in backgrounds
      poring over the edges after   finding where I ended
and others began   saying *is that me?*   *no*
                    there   *is that me?*

     I lost whole nights   to the Glassons sale page
which slid into weeks   then months   then years   until
     whole patches of the cosmos   became blinks of blue light

became an infinite search   through fast fashion at low prices
     for corduroy trousers   with a firm waist
      and lots of room   for child-bearing hips

I have no need for trousers   or hips   anymore
I am bound   to this stained piece of cheap   Swedish furniture
     like Persephone to the underworld   my pockets forever lined
        with pomegranate seeds

my own Pirithous tries occasionally   to untether me   beckons me
     to the bathroom   with the promise   of toothpaste
       or a hot shower but

there will be no hot shower   not in this ghost body
because there is no body   the ectoplasm would drift
                    with the steam
            and anyway
the end remains the same because   there is no end

      it's like taking two left turns   then a right
and circling back   to the same paint-chipped villa
down those stairs   past that tree
            with the house numbers nailed on

only an infinity   of crumpled neck   couch-dwelling
      a big fat fuck you   to evolution
      so

            sorry   to my ancestors
my wide-footed peasants in the Lithuanian fields
            my Middle Eastern ladies   of the sands and seas

they had their klezmer, their livestock   and I have
            whatever this is   this ode to a futon couch
sorry guys
                  this probably isn't
            what you had in mind

my mind is blissfully quite empty   like Nancy Sinatra
      one life for yourself   and one for your dreams

time has stretched
                  so bubble-gum thin

      I'm losing memories   like leaves
the bramble of childhood rivers
      and paddocks of after-school horses
to pat through gaps in the fence are   fading

I am close to forgetting   the summer talent show
where I danced with a friend on an outdoor stage
    to 'Candyman' by Christina Aguilera   in crimson pvc hot pants
that her mum sewed special

the slack-jawed crowd is vanishing
    the way they tried to gauge   our age with narrowed eyes
each scene smudges over with

                    couch couch couch

I'm at a safe distance   on my eternity futon
          never again will I come home   from a night out and
peruse the mental videotape   of every shitty remark
made over a jug
                    because
                    there will be no more nights out

the nights could not be   any more in
                    in is all I know
my futon   is the most in thing   there ever was
      out there   I was   corrosive
licking salt   off the street
      forming crushes   for no good reason

                    nothing like that here
          only cold hard morals

I have seen this house built   and burnt   over and over
          it always ends   the same way

death has come for every person   who has ever died but
          they didn't have this couch, probably

I love my new ghost life   it tastes like earl grey   and the moon
here I am forever soft and plump   and also

                                   neither of those things

      because I am only ectoplasm   if anything
            and now, when heart-sized spiders

      dash through my peripheral vision
I don't even mind   because   nothing
            can touch me here

      I *am* them
                  and they are me, anyway

2

bus poem 3

the bus smells of stale curry   and cigarettes
a guy with new Nikes   and curly gelled hair
          sits still   no headphones, no phone
          just   looking out the window

someone carries
          three totes full of objects
                    with corners

I had a haircut today
and when it was time to blow-dry
                    the hairdresser boosted Phil Collins
          twisted up most of my hair
                    held it with a chopstick
and said   *you know   if I found out tomorrow*
                    that I had like   a terminal illness
          I'd be fine with it cos   this moment, right now
that we're living in   I'm loving what I'm doing   like
          this is what I'm meant to be doing   you know?

and I'm happy with that   I was meant to do hair
                    and we're all just blips like
          on this small blue marble   everyone who has ever lived
and died   has done it on this tiny planet

through the rivers of blood   I mean it   the rivers of blood
          our lives really mean   nothing
                    when you think about it

and I said yeah
maybe that's why people are religious
          so that they have a reason

he pulled apart a knot
and started talking about books
      how books are amazing   because
this thing   that was once a tree   (!)   now holds
the exact thoughts of the writer   *like how many times*
can you say that you were literally in Hitler's head
      and get away with it?

we stewed in this conversation gap
while 'The Killing Moon' played very loudly
I told him this was one of my favourite songs   he told me
that he bought his son special astro-binoculars
        to see that supermoon
    but they missed it
he slapped his thigh
      they fucking *missed it*

he said *you better have somewhere to go tonight because*
    this blow wave is fucking brilliant

I went to a poetry reading
and now   I am on this quiet, sad
                  bus
weaving up up up   like it always does
holding my own hand   so that I don't
    turn on my data
        to see
if you have messaged me

summer

rent money / even after you moved out /
while I collected mugs / rumpled books
sun-faded to Sally Lunn pink / spent Christmas
alone / eating cheap Swiss chocolate and /
smoking out the window / the cherry tomato plant /
staked up by the door stayed dead /
brown / reluctant /

rain so rare / I licked it from my lips /
the Netflix we shared told me / to keep
watching *The Fresh Prince of Bel Air* /
instead I watched blackbirds / thunking
against glass / and watched the sky stay the same /
when they didn't pick themselves up / and fly
back / into the dark night /

taught myself to sleep alone / again /
I tried not to think of / the snow angels we made
in Wanaka / I doubted / what they said about time /
and would've given anything / to flash forward and
see you / today / mashing banana for my baby /
telling me from the kitchen / that you're
in love / and moving to Italy

the only way out of my student loan is to marry ex-FRIENDS star Matthew Perry

in front of the Burbank Garden fountain
James Corden asks the cast   if they still hang out
Matthew Perry says   *nobody talks to me*

they all laugh it off   but he doesn't laugh
I want to nestle him   like a wee lamb
          into my bosom   I want to
feed him tender segments   of mandarin

he needs a gal like me   I'll talk to Matthew Perry
day and night!   he can tell me about his life
as a white man in Hollywood
worth hundreds of millions of dollars

          I can tell him   how I put through pine nuts
                    as peanuts   on the self-checkout

I'm fifty thousand in debt   I know what it's like
          to scrub off mould   that reappears
every two weeks like a curse   I know about *commitment*

maybe we share   a blackened sadness
          maybe his is   calcified   like the placenta
I left at the morgue   until the hospital stopped calling
                    and burnt it with the waste

I might've picked up the phone   if I wasn't
too busy watching   clouds passing   and passing
          in the screen's black reflection

Matthew, do you   collect rainwater too
          in case of emergencies?

do you have someone to call   when you want
to see a movie   and you don't want to go alone?

these days I'm a bit   of a strange brew
        but   I'm willing to descale for you
to wash out my insides   with eight kinds of acid
        till I'm sparkling fresh   white teeth, good bones

Matt, I'll cook you full roast dinners
        I'll collect the wishbones   for a broth of good luck
                is that how it's done?   marriage?
        it'll be like   the opposite of breaking up
over Monopoly   give me your worst, capitalism
        my safe word is   *infrastructure*

it's us against the world, Matty
        I'll whisper
when you're sucking air   through a machine

I'll love you like   people love in a fifties movie
        long kisses in black and white

I'll be . . . . . . there for you
                when the rain
                        turns to acid

when it burns the birds   the trees
the thick dark soil
        and when every mansion
                melts down to soup

marry me (on Runescape)

craft me a   diamond ring
        to keep safe   in my inventory

take me   on a honeymoon
        to a members'-only server

let's make out   in the enchanted valley
        with its thick reeds   its Arctic pines

its pixelated waterfall   only accessible
                via fairy ring

tell me that you're   a twelve-year-old
trumpet player from Colombia   called Victor

                I'll buy it

what if we kissed   in the dungeons?
                ha ha jk

                        unless . . . .

buy me papaya   steal me doughnuts
        from the baker's stall
let me trade   bright food   for jewels

save me   from the dangers   of dragons
        and untethered souls

let me saunter   around the woods
        killing imps   chopping oaks
bake me loaves   of fresh bread
to eat with cheese   and cured meats

let me become   a leggy blonde
        in pink and gold robes   bestow
upon me   your high stat account
                        your paid membership

that you probably bought
                with money you earned
        from your shifts   at Burger King

give me the password   no strings attached
        no long nights texting   unspeakable things

don't be mad   when I bring a friend
to your house after school   for chocolate cake

        I know you didn't just mean   baking

let us knock softly   on the frosted glass door
        in our thick skirts   and sweat-stained blouses

let us unbuckle our leather shoes   to cross
your parents' perfect carpet

don't grip   the kitchen bench   at the sight of us
        just   offer us two slices
wrapped in Glad Wrap   with a shaking hand

                let us go   easy

        I'll give up   the account
the free   rodeo burgers

I'll put in hours   felling trees
        and casting runes   until

I've made my own levels   killed
my own demons   and bought
     the hottest armour   in the village

       I'm self-made   baby

I'm a gorgeous collection   of pixels
     and I'm ready
       to self-destruct

pawn me off   as a prized possession
     sell me   to the wizards

let me become   a chaotic cloud
     ~~~pure chaos energy~~~

     leave me   to the dragons
with low xp   in deep wilderness

I'm into it   break me right
          down

    and build me   back   up

      teleport me   home
        to Lumbridge
feed me   sailfish soup
    brand new   like nothing
     happened

give me   a goblin's last breath
let me watch   its body become
      a pile
   of white bones

I'll either
tuck them neatly   in my backpack

or cast a spell   and turn them
to peaches

cmon

give me your worst
test your morality on me

hack my account
steal   my username

my identity   until
I do not exist

until
I am an internet ghost

the cloudy echo
of a personality

a collection   of cookies

crumbling
slowly
into
cyberspace

Tips for lockdown wellness

let your body know   there is no tiger
        hold yourself close   say *I am safe*
even if the tiger   has let himself in
and is drinking   all the milk in the fridge
then   all the water in the tap
tell yourself   *I am safe*
        even if the tiger is growling
under his breath   that you can't afford
to have the heat pump   on all day
I am safe   even when he brews all the tea
and looks you in the eye
        while it tips to the floor
in a clear black arc
        hold your body close
I am safe   *I am safe*
when his dinner-plate paw   snakes hard
            around your waist
        I am
when he interrupts   your doomscroll
            to suggest that maybe
        you will never   plug
the despondency-shaped   hole
by your liver   *I am safe*
when he leans in close   whispers
one day   *you will watch* Shrek   *for the last time*
and at first you laugh   because you don't even like *Shrek*
but then   you think about it some more and

                fuck

hold yourself close   you are safe
even if   you are actually   engaged
to the tiger   and the registry reads:

Briscoes pillows
a herd of live deer   *Disney Plus*

bake a special brownie   for the tiger
watch the milky fog   of his eyes glazing over
            and when he passes out   draped across the couch
drag his twelve-foot body somewhere secure
and when he wakes up   with a vengeance
            starve him out
                  let him wither away
            let him become a bag of black and orange bones
marooned in the kitchen   the bathroom
the dank little closet
            that backs onto the mud bank
wherever you choose to exile him
don't let him tempt you   with clove cigarettes
or a sexy depression
                  call off the engagement!
let him starve   on the coldest days
while you sit on the recliner chair
by the streaming window
cracking your knuckles   and practising
            magical thinking
trap him in a labyrinth!   show him
                  the real meaning of soul murder
            box him in a room with so many layers
of fleur-de-lis wallpaper that he can barely breathe
take that, tiger!   you asshole
you can find out what it's like
            to know the heave of your ribs
and what it takes   to allow them
            to expand

the things I would do for a Pizza Hut Classic Cheese right now

I would scoop out my eyes   with a spoon
or read all of *Finnegan's Wake* again

I would doggy-paddle   into the Bermuda Triangle
     & be   like
         open to whatever

I would lick the droplets   from the back of a frog
    click my heels & leap
        into a ring of toadstools

one-way ticket   to fairy town, baby!

I would rip the legs off a stick insect   one by one
I would smash my own legs   Kathy Bates-style
    then be forced
       to write a bestselling novel, I guess

I, a black pot, would call the kettle black
I would keep the bathwater   & tip out the baby

I would spit in the face   of a cartoon woodland creature
    as it spun me a dress of sky-blue silk

o, the things we take for granted
o, the freedom we thought we had

I would drink a tank of live sea-monkeys, okay!!!!
I would eat all of the fallen fruit   in my vineyard
I would roar   with the dull weight   of a depressed circus lion

I would climb the mountain I grew up underneath
          in the belly of night   not even stopping
to fill a plastic bottle with the special   mountain water
that Mum used to keep   by the back door
& at the top I would beat my chest   with cold-bitten fists
          then take a piss on the summit snow

I would strip down to my knickers & slither around
          on a backyard Warehouse waterslide   coated
with cheap detergent   on the coldest day of the year

                    hey   I don't even know what day that is!!!
I wouldn't know a day of the week   if it boxed me round the ears currently
o what I would do, what I would give
          almost . . . . . . to a Rumpelstiltskin level   (if u know what I mean)
for a slice of Pizza Hut Classic Cheese

          I would stay loyal to a single
                    New Year's resolution

I would forgive the person
          who hurt me when I was thirteen

just for a glimpse   of that grey-brown box
waiting at my door   like a scorned lover
          or a strange jewel

its shape familiar   among the shit-filled nappies
                    the brown mountain
          of dead leaves

the porch flotsam
of a legally lonely winter

snails

They have been eating the letter addressed to Ban Kupil for weeks. Now the letter is more hole than paper. The snails have eaten the paper and shat it out in long thin ribbons. The long

thin ribbons of paper shit curl into spirals and line the black insides of the mailbox. The snails have been given a new letter to eat. They are nibbling Nicola Willis's face. They are nibbling

Nicola Willis's face and shitting it out in long thin ribbons. Long thin ribbons of Nicola Willis are peppered around the inside of the mailbox like confetti or a cloud of moths swarming

forth from a piñata. At night I shine a torch inside the mailbox and watch the snails gliding over white paper. I can almost see the ribbons of waste emerging underneath them. At night

once the snails have finished eating the letter addressed to Ban Kupil and the one about Nicola Willis they glide out of the mailbox and down the eleven steps and then they take

the path to the right past the tree with my house number nailed on in brass numerals and then they glide along that gravel until they reach the porch with the nappies and strollers and bicycle

at certain times of the day and this is when they glide through the space between door and doorway, along the rimu floor of my downstairs flat, leaving lines of wet silver down the hall

and underneath my bedroom door, and here is where I hear them. I can hear the snails that have eaten the letters. They are saying *corn husk, uproot, biscuit tin*. They are gearing up to ask a very important question. The snails are asking if I've seen the third season of *Twin Peaks*. They think it is kind of derivative especially considering Lynch's notoriety as an auteur

and they're pretty pissed that Special Agent Dale Cooper didn't get the space to make a proper comeback as a character. I whisper back to the snails that I feel the same about Audrey

Horne and in fact kind of think that Sherilyn Fenn maybe forgot how to act but that's okay. The snails agree that what happens in the Black Lodge isn't bound by conventions of time

and space. They agree that creamed corn means pain and sorrow and that stranger things can happen to a teenage girl than an angel disappearing from her bedroom wall painting. This

seems to appease them. They turn back down the hallway and underneath the door and up the stairs into the mailbox, murmuring about Josie in the doorknob, tiny and stuck there forever.

Wasn't it a nightstand-drawer knob? Is Josie okay?
Wasn't she screaming in that last scene?

bat people

Once, in suburbia
selling Girl Guide biscuits,
we found a two-storey house
with no door. No steps,
no ladders, no way in
whatsoever. Only
a large window
on the second level
that opened out
onto nothing. We circled
the house in a thick
disbelief, round
and round until we turned
and walked then ran, the feeling
of being watched tugging
hard at our backs.

bad eggs

I can see the city from up here
        the too-bright billboards
                in blocks of peach & pale lime

      this wind is carving up   the smoke blue
        tide   like birthday cake

all I've done today is buy wine online
& learn about the etymology   of 'bourgeoisie'

I am   sometimes marooned
      on this chopped up sea

stuck   like moss to a log
        or   a leaf-clogged gutter
lodged deep
    like a spoon bent in a litre of ice-cream
           please help

/

think I'll grab some lunch
      maybe a vending-machine lasagne

haven't put on real clothes
        in nearly   four weeks

haven't let myself hope
      that things are slowly
               returning
        to normal
I wouldn't know normal
if it sat on my face

and sang me a Yiddish folk song

the kōwhai are blooming   without me
wait! I've been   pleading
          to the seed pods
wait! don't
          turn into flowers
                    just yet

/

'bourgeoisie' comes from 'burg'
(Frankish; fortification, castle)

          I had a burg last night
                         with chicken so thicc
it was still a lil pink   & jelly-raw
                         in the middle

revolting actually
          but I ate it anyway
like Russian roulette
                         if you really think about it

I've been fighting with my inner critic

my inner critic is constantly
                    rapping my wrists   like a piano teacher
as I round my hands   over the laptop keys
          trying to conjure golf balls
     or eggs   in my palms

my inner critic has Coke-bottle glasses
          and huge tits   like that horrible cliché
                    of the hot librarian

she knows what's good
       and what should go   in the doc
          titled 'scraps'
which sits in the darkest part of the cloud

/

even when I am not marooned
       I am still a little bit at sea
and my brain is full   of bad eggs

a flatmate once asked
      how to check

and when I told him
    he cracked one into a cup of water
        tendrils of egg-white
      swirling
and said *how can I tell*
     if it's floating
       or sinking?

this night's a write-off

nothing good will come from feeling
                                    too inspired
        only fingers that type quicker
                                than the ideas come

the poor ideas left back-straggling   and out of breath   saying
oh my god   please   just stop for a bit   we are actually trying to
        tell you   something cool

the ideas are very overwhelmed
they are maybe even   a bit overstimulated
dressed up in sequins and glitter
        doing shots off each other's taut bellies
then getting out the foghorns and screaming
                        LET'S GET FUCKED UP

they are starting a grassroots movement
it's very   ear to the ground
they are down there   with their ears to the ground
calling themselves   *channels to the other side*
        except they still kind of think that the other side is China

my ideas are rising like the natal sun, like   their star signs
which btw   maybe one is a Cancer   but they're probably all Scorpios
they're a whole matrix of thought   these ideas

they're fascist-killing machines, just like   Woody Guthrie's guitar
        they came up with that first actually
they won't have some white guy take the credit for that one

they are the essence of good weather and the only good thing
to come out of a tidal storm   except for watered plants and salt in the air

they were probably there   at the Chelsea Hotel
     when Patti nursed Robert back to health

my ideas are in the front row of all the good festivals
they were in fact at Woodstock '69
     drinking all the free milk
and crying tears of joy   and catching pneumonia
               their tiny nipples contracting in the cold

my ideas are full bunches of marigolds
they are a flock of Polish-Jew ghosts all set to haunt
the local supermarket, spitting OY VEY
          on single-use plastic and individually wrapped
                    organic energy bars
they are like   if canned meat was a person
they get all dressed up in *Brokeback Mountain* cosplay
just to sit around the house smoking and
          thinking about Linda Cardellini
they are strong teas
and dancing to Miles Davis in the kitchen

               this is all to say that no
          I can't come out tonight
I'd really love to, honestly

but I must stay here   in case they shackle my hands
     to the keyboard   all night long
like a passionate lover
     or a cruel god

revolution

cars are bad and we should replace them with   bats
just fill the streets   with thousands of bats

let bats take you   to your destination
nobody will question your arrival   upon a cloud of bats

we should give the bats terrific ratings   for their services
bump up their credit scores   refer them to a friend

let the bats fly you to   Slovenia
let them cook dumplings   and hot beef soup

let them carry you slowly   like a weathered sedan
your road-trip soundtrack the flap   of a million wings

96 kilometres an hour along roads   where frogs
get frisky   in soggy gutters

let the bats win   instead of the kids
let them lick the morning smear of jam   off your wrist

people are bad and we should replace them   with bats
or at least replace   your partner with bats

find a cave to bunk up   with the bats
bring   your two-cent Matisse prints from Singapore

to hang on the dank cave wall   bring tall ceramic candlesticks
for your romantic   bat dinner dates

where you'll share   organic wine
and loop spaghetti   into tiny mouths

get to know   the bats of your country
the way they clamber   forest floors

on the points   of their wings   like ballet dancers
learn to hunt   beetles, flies, moths

using soft clicks   of echolocation
search for wood roses   the underworld flower

at the feet of trees   drink their nectar
keep the symbiotic   relationship   alive

join a communal roost   practise polyamory
in long-dead trees   dry of wax and sap

think you know bats?   text BATCAVE to 97779
to take the quiz   or plant a tree, kill a possum

keep the cats inside   or join a bat rescue organisation
          please
    please
they're nearly all gone

bus poem 4

bus was cancelled
      I am walking!

a car's windows are so fogged
I'm half expecting to see
Kate Winslet's hand
spread flat
      and sliding

I am listening   to Shocking Blue
they're helping me
      float uphill

a sad-looking man
      in grey polar fleece
is carrying a dozen eggs
    like a firstborn

his eyes widen
     and his mouth sets
as I smile and pass

notches of water
   pulse   in the gutters

four-thirty light
    glides   oil-paint thick
over trees, houses

a girl in a red scarf
is surprised by a voice
     bursting from her phone

our eyes meet
    like a secret
we both know

each leaf's skeleton
  is backlit
the delicate lines
      hold green
flesh tender

a woman in a wool coat
is burying her face in the heads
    of lavender
that sway against a fence

       closer to home
I pass seven
  chicken nuggets
with varying degrees
of oven burn

scattered like ships
across concrete

     one nugget is not
touching the ground
. . . . . . I consider it

bushels of nightshade
crowd the path home

a white basket fungus
sits at their feet

      like a sign
in another language

the sun is out so why am I still depressed?

I would take a pack of Rothmans
and a paperback of *Lolita*
to the fire escape

I would dangle my feet over
the edge as if it was an Italian
balcony or the branch
of an olive tree

but that was then
I don't smoke

and *Lolita* is
        not a fun read

the kawakawa are boasting green
the cabbage trees are spiked with light

it is so lovely actually

even so
        think I'll just

have a look from the window
until the sun
        does that thing again

Calendar Girls

I am wearing a plum satin jumpsuit   with spaghetti straps
      & a silky belt   tied at the waist   the baby is still nestled

deep enough   between my hips   to look like a lunch
we wait for Turkish pizza   baklava   and garlic yoghurt fries

we are at Camel Grill   which we call *Camel Girl*   cos
      it's next to Calendar Girls   and cos   it's cute

we stand   in silence   on the black narrow street   neon signs
      foot traffic   cars blasting beats   until you say

you know, the Calendar Girls actually invented measured time as we know it

I am still cracking up over this   when our food arrives
in its white Styrofoam and silver foil   and even while we eat

          in Pigeon Park darkness   I am even stifling a giggle
in the middle of the Herbie Hancock concert   at Michael Fowler

thinking of the Calendar Girls   in their Neolithic pleaser heels
      their natural shift   to Bronze Age   hair extensions

thick clay glitter   authentic snakeskin print   those girls
who make the world turn   honey, we owe it all   to them

cortisol queen

                                        hey sis
bet u thought u'd seen the last of me

                ur mighty ruler
        queen supreme

                        im here to
        . . . take back the night

sleep? o no
                        no
buckle up, bitch
let's   *hang out*
        let's
                        watch Saturday morning cartoons!

let's listen to the cats   fighting outside
            the noises   like sped-up thunder

let's light a candle   for the ones we've lost
                let's hope they're naked
                            right now
                    and cutting limes for mojitos

let's stay up all night   together!
let's   text   that guy   no
                        the *other* one
            ha ha!

let's think about   the ceiling leaks!
        the books   n cushions
clammy with rainwater

let's watch clips of the opera
                n cry slow fat tears

let's take a dip
        in the *algorithm*

let's bathe in that blue screen glow
            n look up   how long
it would take to varnish
                            a whole castle
let's turn ripe
                to turn rotten
let's think back
                    to running free
        across the peninsula
n know u will never
            do it again

let's lock jaws   around
the meat of the world
                let's thrash until
something
            gives

im here to stir the pot
        to fuck things up

i don't want ur cheap wine
or ur   headspace app

i want u to cry in the shower
        like the crux   of a chick flick
with no romantically based
                resolution at the end

get online, loser
        we're marinating
in our collective trauma!

i want to   waste ur time
                til there's
      nothing left

only dead lemon trees
        n dry toast

only storms
      that batter black coasts
leaving trails

          of loose teeth
    in their wake

stone fruit

his rituals are moon-
bound, ceremonial,

he feasts on peaches,
olives, figs,

he is bathed in a shower
resembling a hot spring

then kneaded
with organic oil

and wrapped
in merino wool,

he is held close, read to,
he curls like a seashell

to hear ocean sounds
or a Joni Mitchell song,

he is laid down, tucked in,
his lamp switched off

and curtains drawn to block
morning light

and he sleeps
little prince,

the one who wasn't planned
but wasn't unexpected.

pumpkins

mesmerised by a busker
he rakes the crate for a ripe tamarillo
as we line up to buy an armful
of oranges, kumara, kale

on the island next to mine
before I knew he existed
his world was alive   with fog
and frosted windscreens

tucked in a banana box, he slept
on the street, weeks old
dark hair pooling into cardboard shadow
while his dad sold jade and silver necklaces
on those black nineties cords

when he was thirteen he gave his dad a small egg
laid by the whitest hen
with a letter saying *thank you*   *for your endless love*

reading it I wanted to cry
but the feeling belongs to him   if he wants it

though it feels like we share a life
its bills, bed, children,
            we are still   in parallel,
sometimes back
   on different islands

he pays for the produce with coins
and drops change in the busker's hat

a young man slices pumpkins   with a long blade
that arcs through the air

the man's muscles are taut   under a white singlet
sweat is beading blue on his skin

Emma and Rodney's sunroom

Rodney says: *sometimes I take a chair to the open window and pretend I'm flying*

       but you aren't going anywhere? I counter
he takes a long drag   gives me a look

      in socks, cane chairs   and Kilbirnie darkness
we smoke joints and look at stars

Rodney did a ten-day meditation retreat north of Auckland
         there was lots of porridge   and back pain

I turn to the birdhouse
           down on the lawn
        the moonlit magnolia
       the strangeness of these
     seaside suburbs   all burrowed in hills
but somehow so flat

shall we go inside? says Emma
once we've gone from the Kubrick canon   to those octopuses
        that drag themselves up the beach

our lips have turned dry

     Emma's about to put a whole bag
       of chicken nuggets in the oven

soon we'll pool the leftover tequila and beer
    into a red solo cup   and take turns
till we're on the carpet
          looking up at party lights
      like they're satellites
       spelling out messages

in a minute

a plane is passing
I close my eyes
and lean my body halfway out
the sunroom window

cow fund

was it   Pams Finest Kapua Double Cream Brie
          or Waimata Sheep Milk Camembert
or Whitestone's Creamy Havarti
that I ate
while stoned at book club?
it was probably something artisan
          from Moore Wilson's

                                        fuck

          I'll never know

maybe I should put aside $5 a week
for years and years
          until I have enough
                    to buy my own cow

I'll milk her
          in the pink dawn
add bacteria
          then rennet
                    to the warmed harvest
                              then wait

          all the while
                    remembering
the exact mouthfeel
          of that perfect   soft cheese
on a fig and olive   cracker

the fresh   top notes   the sweet goopy
          middle   the way it clung

my new savings account
          is called *cow fund*

I'll buy her when I've saved enough   to comfortably
         feed the ducks   Blue Frog Granola
my cow and I will be very happy together

we will have a symbiotic relationship
like   I had with the cows of my youth

                who were peaceful
       in their paddocks
while I pissed beside their pats   at 4am
reeking of whiskey   mud in my ponytail
       this time
I'll do it right

I will shampoo my cow
        until her coat   froths up soft

I will run my hands
        through her tufts
             glittering
velveteen under
       arcadian meadow sun

I will sing   Simon and Garfunkel
       my cheek pressed to hers
as we doze on clover and daisies

I will gaze into her eyes until
       we melt against each other

comparing the scars we can see
        and the ones we can't

all we'll have is   each other

I'll think up a memoir
      about my new bovine life
            called something like
                  My Years of Horns and Udders
    or   *Those Who Weep in the Cornfields*
                      like
          those based-on-a-true-story movies
where someone escapes
          to the Alaskan wilderness
in an anti-capitalist rage

      hunting moose and losing
            all their good teeth

                        till they eat   the wrong perennial herb
      and starve to death
          in a sun-baked caravan

maybe, after all
      I won't even milk her

especially if she has a calf one day
she'll need that for her baby

      maybe I'll help with delivery
arms gloved and lubed
        way up in the birth canal

        as her doula, her guide
    I'll offer something deeper
than words of encouragement   I'll offer
      fertile courage
        cosmic energy

then, in the earthy afterglow

we'll lie back   the three of us

I'll point out Venus   and the best constellations
          I'll wonder if she   wishes
                    for comets   like me

or if she wonders
                    about anything

I won't even need cheese
          I'll nestle into her toffee-coloured coat

same as every dusk for years
                              and know
                              that this is all there is

walking to book club

early, even after looking at silverbeet
through the community
garden fence,

after breathing jasmine air
near houses painted gold
and cornflower blue,

on streets where a Shirley Barber fairy
might guide lost rabbits home
by the light of her bluebells,

I saw a man lead a small girl
and her pink bicycle
through a latched gate,

past a front-yard lemon tree
and into the waiting arms
of a woman

who steered her inside
then turned back to the man,
her face blooming as she held his

Country Music

(after 'Snakes and Waterfalls' by Nick Shoulders)

There's a song you think I'll like.
We watch the video, where a man
in the forest yodels and whistles
and sings about Louisiana, his dog
panting happily for four whole minutes.
I like it. A lot, actually. I watch it
six more times later, when I'm alone
and the house breathes with sleep
and dark. I want to love somewhere
this much, every tree and cave and
lake, like this white mulleted man,
his heart in his voice like an offering.
The next morning I suggest moving
to the American South. You laugh
and laugh and laugh and I look
at the oak tree outside
full of kākā and tūī singing.

Notes

Some of these poems have first homes: 'spawning season', 'Last Call Nigel' and 'Country Music' can be found in *Starling*; 'I am the ghost of the IKEA futon couch' and 'Memphis Belle' in *Food Court*; 'marry me (on Runescape)' and 'guided hypnosis' in *Sweet Mammalian*; 'the things I would do for a Pizza Hut Classic Cheese' in *Stasis*; and 'Clucky' in *Milly Magazine*. Versions of 'all the leaves are brown and my heart is a free-range egg' appear in *Mayhem* and the Compound Press 2022 Poetry Calendar. A big thank you and much gratitude to these journals for supporting my work and the work of so many others.

'masterclass' references the 1969 Pink Floyd album *Ummagumma*, particularly the track 'Several Species of Small Furry Animals Gathered Together in a Cave and Grooving with a Pict'.

'"Patched gang members in the Māori Affairs Committee Room", 1979' is in response to a photograph of the same name as part of the 'Encountering Mīharo' exhibit at the National Library in early 2021. The photograph is by Ans Westra. Ref: AW-1820. Alexander Turnbull Library.

'0800 SEE ORCA' is in response to the passing of Toa the orca, who was stranded on Plimmerton Beach in July 2021.

'Snails': Ban, I'm really sorry that the snails ate your letter.

Acknowledgements

Thank you to the IIML poetry and creative nonfiction MA class of 2021 for being such attentive and generous readers – to Dani Yourukova, Bronte Heron, Flora Feltham, Zoe Higgins, Maggie Sturgess, Scarlett McAvinue-Northcott, Sylvan Spring, Jiaqiao Liu and especially Lachlan Taylor, with whom I shared a great deal of coffee and quizzes while we wrote our work together. All that laughter has found its way in here, thanks to you.

Thank you to Chris Price for offering insightful feedback and being a constant support throughout the year. Thank you to Francis Cooke, Louise Wallace and the wider *Starling* team, who have platformed my and so many other young writers' work for years now. It is an honour to be a part of the growing *Starling* community.

Special thanks is due to the brilliant high school English teachers who witnessed my teenage poetry. To Tony Beyer, Judith Lamb and the late Chris Bates – thank you for the early encouragement and for taking young people seriously. To my parents, too, who kept it a well-hidden secret if they ever wished that I'd studied law or med – thank you.

Thank you to poetry club for the inspiration and kindness and karaoke. To Ella, Jordan, Stacey, Rebecca, Ash, Sinead, Alayne and the many others who frequent a song or a BYO every now and then – you guys are the best.

Acknowledgment is also due to the (super uncomfortable) futon couch on which I wrote a large part of this book, and to the numerous delivery drivers who climbed down a hundred steps in the dark just to drop off a pizza by a pile of pooey nappies when I was in crisis mode and Really Needed One . . .

Thank you to Asa for being the coolest baby (and now toddler, barely) to ever exist on the face of this crumbling planet, and mostly, thank you to Jasper, for working through nights and parenting through days while I was out writing poems. Thank you for all that you did and continue to do so that I can keep faith in writing.